The Great Escaper

Library of Congress Number: 78-26629

1   2   3   4   5   6   7   8   9   0   83   82   81   80   79

Printed and bound in the United States of America.

Library of Congress Cataloging in Publication Data

Warren, David.
  The great escaper.

  SUMMARY: Relates the dramatic stage life of
magician and escape artist Harry Houdini.
  1.   Houdini, Harry, 1874-1926 — Juvenile literature.
2.   Magicians — United States — Biography — Juvenile literature.   [1.   Houdini, Harry, 1874-1926.   2.   Magicians]
I.   Large, Annabel.   II.   Title.
GV1545.H8W37   793.8'092'4 [B] [92]   78-26629
ISBN 0-8393-0152-9 lib. bdg.

The Great Escaper

By
David Warren

Illustrations by
Annabel Large

Raintree Publishers
Milwaukee • Toronto • Melbourne • London

Harry Houdini was one of the greatest escape artists of all time. He could free himself from almost anything — handcuffs, leg chains, ropes, milk cans, packing crates, coffins, and straitjackets.

Houdini's real name was Ehrich Weiss. He was born in Hungary and grew up in New York City. By the time he was 16 he had a steady job in a factory. He spent his free time learning to do magic tricks with cards and handkerchiefs. He was short and powerful and a strong swimmer. Soon he became interested in escapes. He would get people to tie him up and then practice freeing himself. He learned to pick locks and to make tiny skeleton keys, which he hid on his body.

When Houdini was 17, he became a full-time performer. He did magic tricks and escaped from rope-ties.

"Do you expect to make a living like that?" asked his mother. Later, when he was world famous, he asked to be paid in gold and gave the coins to his mother.

For a long time Houdini was just
another struggling performer. His act
was not polished, and he had not learned
to make his escapes look difficult. In
1894 a tiny woman called Bessie
Raymond joined his act. She was very
small and light, the ideal size for curling
up inside the false compartments of his
magic-box trick. Soon Bessie Raymond
and Harry Houdini were married.

They traveled together for 32 years. They went from theater to theater. They had very little money. One night, when they were cold and hungry, they cooked potatoes on a fire made from an old packing case.

As Houdini broke the box apart, he got an idea. Later he used a packing case in one of his most famous escape acts.

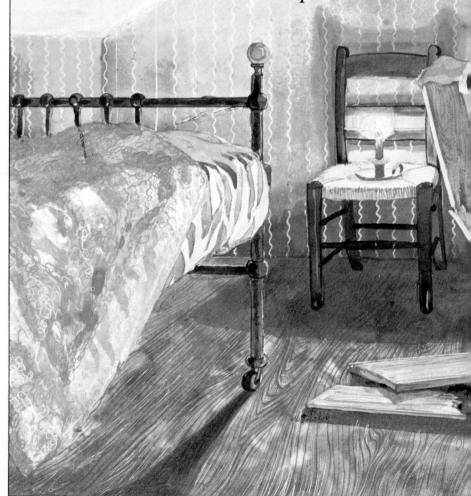

9

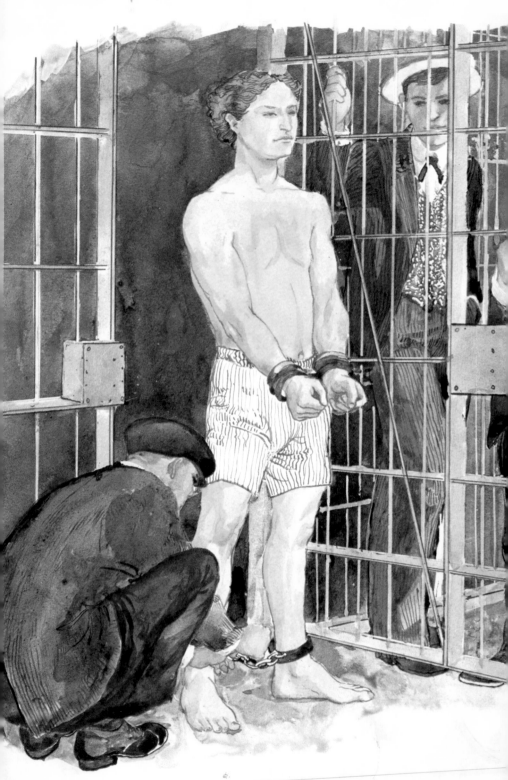

Houdini soon learned to get free
publicity for his escapes. He would
challenge the local police to handcuff
him and lock him in one of their cells.
He always got out, and the newspapers
were full of reports of his escapes. It
looked like magic, but actually Houdini
was just very clever and paid great
attention to details. He would smuggle in
tiny tools or get an impression of the
keys on a blob of wax.

One day a theater manager told Houdini, "Your act is terrible, son. You're crowding too much into it."

"Forget the magic," continued the manager, "and stick to the escapes." This was good advice, and Houdini took it.

In 1900 the Houdinis went to Europe. In Germany, Harry decided to jump into a river after being locked into handcuffs, chains, and leg irons. "Forbidden," said the police. But Houdini jumped in anyway. He stayed underwater as long as he could. Just when the crowd thought he had drowned, he popped up again.

13

Houdini did many of his escapes in curtained cabinets. However, he did some of his acts in full view of the audience. This was how he got out of a straitjacket. He escaped without any trickery — just great strength and skill.

Sometimes, strapped into a straitjacket, he hung by his ankles from a skyscraper. Actually, it was easier to get out that way because in order to free himself, he had to get his arms above his head. Hanging head downward made it easier. Audiences loved this act.

Houdini escaped from his famous "Impregnable Box" inside a curtained cabinet on stage. The nails on one side were short, so he could open the box from the inside with a tiny jack. Once outside the box, he quickly replaced the nails while the orchestra played loudly to drown the noise.

In Russia, Houdini nearly came to his end. He was challenged to escape from the dreaded carette, a steel cart used to transport prisoners. Houdini had a look and found the bottom of the carette was made of zinc, which is much softer than steel. He made two small tools to cut through it. One was like a can opener, and the other was a steel coil with saw teeth. But before Houdini was ready, the Russians stripped him and searched him for tools; then they put him into the carette. Houdini was trapped. Not even he could escape from an all-metal prison with only his bare hands.

"Please let me say goodbye to Bess," he begged. The Russians agreed. Bess pressed her face to the tiny window. Their lips met in a kiss — and Bess passed him the tools. The rest was easy.

Houdini prepared carefully for every escape. One cold winter day, he decided to jump into the Detroit river. "I shall jump from the bridge bound with chains and handcuffs," he announced. The authorities pointed out that the river was frozen.

"Then cut a hole in the ice. I am Houdini!"

He made his jump. But he was swept under the ice before he could free himself. Later he told reporters that he breathed the air bubbles under the ice until he reached the hole again. The truth is that Houdini had a safety line tied around his waist. Even though he was brave, he never left anything to chance.

Houdini handled publicity very cleverly. One of his most famous escapes was from a packing case in New York harbor. Inside the case, Houdini was chained and handcuffed. Then the packing case was thrown into the water. For several days Houdini had practiced escaping from this case in a swimming pool. The case had special screws and concealed hinges. Houdini could open one side with a thin strip of steel.

When Houdini was ready, he told the newspapers what he planned to do. Crowds lined the dock as Houdini got ready for the stunt. Then the police came bustling up.

"What's going on here?" they asked. Houdini explained about his act.

"You can't do that here! No one is allowed to jump off the New York pier, box or no box," the police said.

"All right," said Houdini, "we'll hire a boat." He signaled to a tug and loaded the box and chains on it. He invited the reporters standing around to join him on board. Then the tug sailed for the harbor mouth. One reporter was left behind. He jumped into the water and swam after the boat until it stopped and he was hauled aboard.

Once out in the bay, Houdini asked the reporters to examine the handcuffs and chains and lock them on him. The reporters examined the box too, before they nailed it shut with Houdini inside. Then the box was dropped into the water.

For 57 seconds, the reporters held their breath. Then up bobbed Houdini and they burst into cheering. After that, the New York newspapers were full of stories about Houdini's underwater escape.

25

One of Houdini's most thrilling escapes was from the Water Torture Cell. Houdini hung head down in a glass-fronted tank of water. His ankles were locked into the frame at the top of the tank. The people in the audience held their breaths as the curtains closed. The minutes passed. Finally Houdini popped out from behind the curtains, wet but triumphant.

To this day nobody knows for sure how he did that trick. Some people believe that the catches on the ankle locks would come apart when the water reached a certain level. But one thing is sure. There were two valves at the bottom of the tank. If anything went wrong, Houdini could have quickly turned the valves and let the water out.

Few people could hold their breath as long as Houdini could. But they often tried to when he used water in his escapes on stage. In one act Houdini crouched in a milk can filled with water while the orchestra played "Asleep in the Deep." The curtains closed. A big clock on the theater wall ticked off the minutes. One . . . two . . . three. People's lungs were bursting. Then Houdini appeared — free! It was a trick can, of course, but it was an exciting stunt.

Houdini's death was as dramatic as his life. In Montreal he was accidentally hit very hard in the stomach. Although he was in terrible pain, he kept on working. A few days later in Detroit, he saw a doctor.

"You need an operation," said the doctor. "You must go to the hospital at once."

"The show must go on," said Houdini. And it did, though his temperature was very high. Just before the end of the show he collapsed. He died several days later and was buried in a coffin that he had once used for his escapes.